MW00809444

me to see my faith and hope for the things God promised me. My overall wholeness came from knowing that I was not designed to be perfect and that not being perfect is okay. It came from knowing that God isn't as hard on me as I am on myself. My wholeness came from believing in myself despite what my past had taught me. My spiritual journey has taught me that I had to get down to the root and start processing and healing what had been holding me back. I had to learn to love myself in order to allow love to love me back, and most of all, I have learned to be resilient, unapologetically.

2 Corinthians 4:8-9 (ESV) "We are afflicted in every way, but not crushed; perplexed, but not driven to despair; persecuted, but not forsaken; struck down, but not destroyed;"

people at a young age to stop them from fulfilling their purpose on this earth." But I decided that my purpose was far too important to let it be stopped because of my trauma. I needed to be like an eagle and soar above it all. It was not easy, but I have learned that life is more fulfilling when we chase the storm rather than run from it. I love the idea of dancing in the rain rather than running to hide from it. When I think of dancing in the rain, I think of an unveiling of what you are hiding. Stay in the rain long enough, and the makeup will wash off while who you are will remain. The storm cleanses us and allows us to be vulnerable. Vulnerability gives us the ability to show who we really are sometimes. I learned the most about myself, not in those good moments, but in those bad ones. I learned how to be a better wife from my failed marriage. I learned how to be a better listener and communicator from those moments when I was not heard. I learned to be a better mother from having a meltdown when my baby cried all day. I learned to be a better friend from those who treated me poorly. There are so many lessons I have learned through my bad experiences that just like the eagle, I would rather experience the storms than run away from them. If I would have run from the storm, I would not be an author today. I would not be a clinical counselor or own several businesses. The storm has taught me to love again, and I am now a wife and a loving mother. In order to get to where you want to be, you have to get through the storm so you *can* be. My journey hasn't been an easy one. Many experiences I've faced left me broken and have taken me to some low places. Through it all, my journey has been one of resilience. The only way I got to where I am today was through faith, hope, and resilience. My faith is what kept me strong. Hope gave me another chance, and my resilience allowed

Unapologetically Resilient

A guide to getting through trauma
and living your full potential

Laurine LeBlanc

Contents

Dedication

I would like to first dedicate *Unapologetically Resilient* to God. I know that this is one of the things He wanted me to accomplish, which is assisting people in moving past trauma and getting to their full potential. I would like to thank my mom for always teaching me that I am able to do anything I believe in. To my Literary BAE, Tiffany Williams, thank you so much for understanding my story and seeing my vision. It was easy to work with you, and this will not be the last time. To Sharai Robbin, thank you for delivering on your promise and helping me along the way with making my dream to be an author come true. To my friends that challenged me, prayed for me, inspired me and motivated me along the way, thank you.

Thank you to my amazing significant other, ElDon, and my wonderful children, Aamir, Anya and ElDon the II. To all my family and friends, I love you dearly. I am sure that I would not be where I am today without you all giving me a reason to grow.

Introduction

My shaking little palms pounding on the slammed shut door did very little to stop the vicious attacks from my step cousins. As water filled my eyes and tears bounced off my rosey cheeks, I did not understand what I had done to deserve such harsh treatment. My unanswered cries for help were met by harsh treatment from my step aunt. *Does she know her sons are hurting me?* Not being able to formulate the words to tell my mom what was going on made it seem like I was a spoiled child that just did not like to be dropped off. Approaching my step aunt's house every morning was like knowing I was going to the electric chair that very moment, not knowing what to do to sway the "evil one" from literally taking my innocence. I lived with the fear and terror of knowing that no one would save me from my "family."

I learned early on: the people you trust the most can be the people that hurt you the most. Trust can be broken, and this will have an impeding effect on how you form and develop relationships. It may also affect how you see God. My relationships were strained. I learned that people could be cold and calculating. Of course, my relationships with men were strained early on due to not having an example of what a good man looked like. To me, all men had an ulterior motive and since I looked at God as a man, he did too.

My mother had to be both man and woman, and she was just that. She taught me love, intellect, hard work and perseverance. But I didn't learn what a healthy relationship was because I didn't see it. The physical abuse I witnessed from my mother's significant others had a daunting effect on me, and it took a long time to get past it.

Generational cycles have a way of circling around. The cries of my mother became my cries; the abuse of my mother became my abuse. One day I looked into my daughter's eyes, praying that my cries would not become hers. The look of disgust I had on my face when I saw my mother allow men to physically abuse her became the same look I gave myself when I allowed the same harm to happen to me. It felt too familiar.

"That will never be me," I told myself, only to find that I was becoming a duplicate. My mother's heartache became mine because that generational cycle was not broken. Sometimes, the best teacher is the example of what you allow and what you see. That's why it is not surprising to see a demon or an evil spirit attached to a sinning parent that jumps and transfers into the children, which forms a curse line. When we do not get a hold of these evil spirits, they will be attached to us for life. There is no secret that alcoholics have a higher chance of producing children that end up on alcohol, and adults that are mentally ill will likely end up producing children that have a mental illness. It's a vicious cycle. You start to notice that you mirror the liar you hated. You start to see yourself in the people that have taught you mistrust. In the midst of mistrust, there's manipulation, and with that manipulation, you start to believe that manipulation is needed in order to protect you from you.

Cycles may be so vicious that we question God. *"Why put this on me?"* But once you start living, you start to understand exactly why you went through the adversities you went through. As you begin to live--and I mean truly live--you start to learn that it was all a part of God's divine plan. The unfairness starts to look and feel like a blessing. The unworthiness starts to feel like you are more than worthy. The hopelessness starts to feel and look like hope. My theory is that the rougher your beginning, the more blessed you will end up, but that is only when you decide to follow God and allow Him to use you.

When you get to the point where you realize that the people that have hurt you were hurt and lost themselves, you're close to healing. The abuser was most likely abused. The molester was most likely molested. The person who showed you hate didn't know love. You begin to understand that the person's hate towards you has little to do with you and more to do with them. We all have some inner work to do. Without doing this inner work, we tend to hurt the people we are supposed to love. My inner work was me recognizing that I was still carrying around this 4-year-old that was raped, molested, and physically and emotionally harmed. I recognized the damaged version of myself was protecting me from myself. She would constantly remind me that people are not trustworthy. She would remind me that I was not deserving of love,and that I was not valuable. When I realized that the 4-year-old me was hindering my progress, I had to learn to use her in the right ways, not the ways that were damaging to me. I never totally let her go. I just learned how to live appropriately with her.

This book will give you an opportunity to learn how to forgive, heal, and focus on inner healing. This book will help you understand self-care versus self-love and how setbacks can be a setup for success. No matter what adverse experiences you face in life, it doesn't mean you're broken. In fact, it means you are gaining an armour of strength to defeat other battles that will come.

CHAPTER 1

Trauma: Your Brain, Your Thoughts, Your Actions

*T*hose who have experienced any form of physical, emotional, or sexual trauma are typically changed forever. Not only does it affect how they see the world, but it affects how they see themselves. Researchers have stated that trauma victims feel a sense of unworthiness in this world that may hinder some from reaching their full potential. I had my own struggles with feeling unworthy and not feeling like I deserved respect because I wasn't given respect in so many ways. At times, the trauma pushed me to be better than anyone expected. But there was a part of me that wanted to submit to failure. I would revert to negative behaviors that resembled the trauma.

There are times that victims of trauma are fixated at the age the abuse occurred. For instance, if the abuse happened at age five, it is not uncommon for the victim to behave, emotionally, like a 5-year-old into adulthood. The traumatic event leaves victims feeling burdened by shame and feeling as though they were the reason why the abuse occurred. Besides having internal scars from trauma, it also has an adverse effect on the brain.

The four main areas of the brain that trauma affects are the hippocampus, the amygdala, the prefrontal cortex, and the brain stem. The hippocampus is a small, curved formation in the brain that plays an important role in the limbic system. The limbic system is the area of the brain that stores memory and emotions. The hippocampus is involved in the formation of new memories and is also associated with learning and emotions. Trauma has a way of not allowing the individual to formulate new memories properly. They may be reliving the traumatic event often, which makes it hard to create new and healthy memories.

The amygdala is responsible for processing emotions. Those who have traumatic experiences have issues with properly processing emotions. In fact, when something triggers their emotions in the wrong way, it can bring them back to the traumatic event. When something brings them back to that traumatic event, they are now in survival mode. When they feel threatened, the brain signals the body to release stress hormones including cortisol and adrenaline. Studies have found that when victims experience trauma, they may have other mental issues as well, such as anxiety and/or depression.

Anxiety is an anticipation of something negative happening. Anxiety may lead to panic attacks which is when neurons are sending the wrong messages to the brain, making the person feel as if they are in fight or flight mode. When we do not properly deal with trauma, trauma has a way of dealing with us. It took me a long time to realize that I had to work through some traumatic issues from my past. Not properly working through these issues resulted in dealing with anxiety.

Once, when I went to the hospital, I asked the doctor to check my heart. After he checked everything, he asked me what was going on in my mind. *"Your heart is fine,"* he said, because my heart *was* fine. That's when I knew I was suffering from anxiety attacks.

For a long time, I was carrying around that physical, sexual, and emotional abuse from childhood and the weight of it all, and it finally hit me. I was constantly worried about something negative happening, whether it be me failing or being attacked in some way again, until one day I was picked up from the ground after having a panic attack while working as a substitute teacher. I remember saying a prayer to God. I said, *"Please don't let me die here,"* because in my mind, I felt I was having a heart attack.

This is why the effects of traumatic experiences are difficult to disassociate from. We embody this with what we truly are. We forget that no matter what we have experienced or what we are carrying, we are perfect in God's image. God's vision for our life is to be great and meant to be in his image. Since we are made in God's image, His vision for our lives is for us to be great.

As humans, our thinking process interferes with consciously being able to separate our misfortunes and mistakes from what we are meant to be. It's almost like a pregnancy, but not with a child. We go through the embedding of trauma (the traumatic event or events), we give it life through our thoughts, and then we carry it until we eventually give birth to it through the manifestation of behaviors associated with the trauma. Maybe someone who has been abused becomes the abuser. Or someone who has been verbally attacked starts to attack people instead of communicating effectively. We are no longer operating in our full potential in Christ. We are now operating through fear and pain. Our fear and pain becomes a part of our aura. If we do not become aware of our aura or energy, this is what we will embody. This is what we will unconsciously attract into our lives.

Romans 14:22 (NIV) " So whatever you believe about these things keep between yourself and God. Blessed is the one who does not condemn himself by what he approves."

CHAPTER 2

Relationships

How we see and identify with the world is deeply rooted in our history, history that is passed down through generations and through distant generational patterns, even rooted in karma or curses. This history is constructed by our experiences, and the trials and tribulations we have experienced or that have been passed down to us through generational spirits. When we experience life changing events or traumas, they become a part of us. We adopt it and carry it until we have the courage to let go of it and create our own identities, breaking generational patterns and praying away the curses from our history.

Deuteronomy 24:16 (NKJV) "Fathers shall not be put to death for their children, nor shall children be put to death for their fathers; a person shall be put to death for his own sin."

Sometimes there's an uncertain smile and unassurance that follows us because of our history. I know for me there was an echoing of "not worthy enough" or "not good enough". Most days it felt like people were staring at my imperfections and pulling me apart piece by piece, leaving me to feel incomplete. I wasn't whole.

I didn't have full awareness as a toddler that it wasn't my fault--the molestation, the rape, and the betrayal. I felt like a puzzle piece that just did not fit in a family frame.

The trauma from my childhood caused me to be delayed. My mother, being an immigrant, not knowing much English, had its setbacks. Because she didn't know much English, I had a hard time learning the English language, and I was kept back in kindergarten as a result. Even as a young, naive 5-year-old, I understood the concept of not doing well and being left behind. Repeating kindergarten fueled my belief that I was inadequate. I carried that feeling throughout grade school. I felt I wasn't good enough, and that feeling echoed in my life until I reached college. I had a teacher in middle school pull me to the side one day and ask me if I was okay because I seemed to be extremely behind, but the truth was I did not want to try. Her tone and the way she treated me made me feel like even more of a failure.

It is human nature to see flaws in people, but God does not see flaws in us. The Bible says, in **Song of Solomon 4:7 (NIV), "You are altogether beautiful, my darling; there is no flaw in you."** In God's eyes, we are all beautiful. In my mother's eyes, I was beautiful as well. In my eyes I was a monster. The ugliest person I had ever seen was looking right back at me in the mirror. I would often look at the popular girls in school and wish I was them. I would dream of miraculously one day being beautiful in hopes that I could stop being bullied at school. But to my dismay, I would run to the mirror in disappointment because I looked the exact same way I did the day before. I was still a skinny girl with big glasses, braces, and an afro. I was not accepted because of my appearance. I even experienced being the subject of pranks. I recall picture day when someone put something in my hair and it was captured in the school's yearbook that year. I also remember a "friend" telling me that my secret admirer was waiting for me on the playground just for me to go outside and be locked outside by myself.

I wasn't accepted, so I would be the class clown. Being the class clown didn't stop them from saying I had the cooties and that they would get dirty if they touched me. This caused a great deal of insecurity which made my self-worth plummet lower than before. From that experience I birthed the complex of people pleasing. I believed that this would help me with being bullied, but it didn't stop it. It did give me some attention, though.

The bullying went on for a few years. Then, I grew into myself. It was my sophomore year of high school. Soon, the braces came off and the glasses turned into contacts and just like that I was a new "beautiful girl". My features were more noticeable without the glasses and I now had a straight smile. My afro, now pressed and straight, gave me more of an "acceptable" look at the time. I now ran to the mirror with excitement, but with a little bit of fear that I would magically not be attractive anymore or accepted. I, of course, still had the same unresolved insecurities. Those insecurities became a part of me. I held onto those insecurities so tightly that they became a part of my aura. Even though I knew I was outwardly pretty, I still felt a sense of inadequacy. The inadequacy showed in how I interacted with people. I would always seek validation. There was always something I would wear, or a hairstyle I would try to be noticed. My feelings of inadequacy either attracted people and friends that felt inadequate too, or people who felt a sense of empowerment because my inadequacy fueled their spirits and they felt better about themselves. We attract what we feel about ourselves, whether we know it or not.

Transitioning from being bullied to gaining attention, I developed the spirit of vanity. Throughout high school, I struggled to maintain good grades due to being preoccupied with my outside appearance. Walking down the hallway with this new appearance meant more attention, and I loved it, but that meant I had to work hard at maintaining the look. I got a job after school solely to keep up with the wardrobe and new hairstyles I wanted. I had to be able to pay for it myself if my mom would say no. My newfound confidence gave me an ego, but there was still a shyness because my outward appearance did not change how I felt about myself deep inside. Socially, I became a little more known than I was before, and that's what I cared about.

My grades suffered. My mother always instilled the importance of hard work in me. Although I didn't fully believe in myself, my mother did. She basically told me that if I did not complete high school and go to college, I would not have a place to stay. Although I lacked the grades to get into college, God sent an angel my way—my guidance counselor. She looked at me and told me that I would make it to college even though I only had a 2.0 GPA. After having someone believe in me, I promised myself that if I made it to college, I would do my best and actually open up a book. A school took a chance on me. It was Cheyney University, the first historically black college or university (HBCU) in the United States of America.

The night before I was to leave for college, I was excited. I was packing my clothes for school when my mom's husband walked in my room. He was in a drunken rage. He said, *"I don't know why you're going to college. You will never be shit!"* My sadness quickly turned into frustration and anger. After our screaming and cussing match, I cried myself to sleep, thinking, *What if I fail?* I was determined not to!

The first year at Cheyney, I made all A's. I found that when I actually believed in myself, I could do well. I found that what I was missing in my past was effort. In the past, I did not put any effort into myself because for so long I didn't believe I would succeed. Cheyney changed my life! What I learned was that I always had the spirit of success inside of me, but it was up to me to activate it. My father was successful, and I had ancestors that were doctors, and dentists, and who worked for the government, but I didn't tap into my abilities until I started truly wanting and began seeking a better version of myself.

The Awakening

My sophomore year, I met, at the time, who I believed was my soulmate, but my soul wasn't ready. He was an attractive, multi-talented musician, dancer, and basketball player. We hit it off immediately. We met at the school cafeteria, and after that, we were inseparable. We experienced a lot of firsts together. Traveling, looking for apartments, and visiting each other's parents' houses for dinner. At that time, I saw my future in him, but I didn't realize how much work I had to do. The awakening occurred, because in that relationship, I learned the most about myself--what I needed, how I needed to grow, and what things needed to improve.

I was still battling issues from my past, unresolved issues that were buried and unbothered until meeting him awakened it. For instance, I did not know I had anger issues and a short temper, or that I could be violent, until I tried to love someone. In that relationship, a lot of the things I witnessed growing up was who I became. He was patient; I was quick-tempered, like a ticking time bomb waiting to explode. Many times, we don't know we have issues until we have to be faced with them. This was when I knew I needed help dealing with some of the traumatic issues I had experienced.

I believed I could love this man the way he needed to be loved, but I failed, because at the time, I didn't know what real love looked like. I had no positive model to follow. It seemed that my academic life and career were on an upward spiral, but my relationship was on a downward spiral, and quickly. All the things that I believed were in my past—the abuse, the molestation, the feelings of inadequacy—quickly manifested when I met my soulmate. The once victim became the victimizer. I became physically and emotionally abusive. Not only did my inadequacies become prevalent, but they assisted in launching my sense of self-discovery, a self-discovery that would take years to attain and mold.

The love affair was rocky, essentially from the start, but that didn't stop life from happening. I ended up pregnant at the beginning of my junior year of college and had to drop out. Initially, we were both excited, because even through the course of our unhealthy relationship, we still envisioned our lives together. But after the initial reaction of excitement, it all quickly turned into resentment because I felt like I had failed again. At the time, I felt I had become another statistic: a college drop-out, unmarried, with a baby on the way. The disappointment in my mother's face when I returned home caused me great grief. She literally cried for three days straight. Her tears made me feel like a major disappointment. I felt like a failure because honestly, all I wanted to do is make my mother proud. I understood her pain and felt her pain. We did not speak during that time because watching the initial response was too much for me. My mother eventually opened back up and helped me through my first pregnancy. I recall her taking me to the local social services center because I had to apply for medicaid, WIC, and food stamps. I remember her looking at me saying, *"I never thought you would be on stamps."* I felt my heart sink in because I never believed I would either.

At that time, I suffered a great deal of depression and anxiety, especially after our son, a beautiful baby boy named Aamir, was born. I had pressure to prove myself wrong. I had to be successful because people were rooting against me. So, immediately after I had my son, I went back to college, but the pressure of succeeding caused me a great deal of anxiety, which resulted in panic attacks. Once, a panic attack was so bad that I fell on the ground at school and people had to pick me up. I went to the hospital and told the doctor to check my heart. He said there was nothing wrong with my heart and asked what was going on in my mind. That's when I knew I was suffering from anxiety.

The relationship with my son's father became a constant back and forth. We eventually got married, and then we divorced because we were growing apart and we did not have a firm, sturdy foundation to begin with. I became engulfed in my career and he would get part-time jobs that he would barely keep. At some point, my success became a point of resentment for him. That relationship taught me to keep discovering who I am.

Throughout my years of self-discovery, I had to ask myself

questions like, *Why do I react the way I do toward someone who wants to love me? Why don't I know the proper response to love? Which one of my ancestors do I have to blame for the things I'm dealing with right now?*

During my self-discovery, I had the ability to expect great things even when things did not look the way I thought it should have looked at the time. Of course, I had some anxieties and fears, but ultimately, I knew that no matter what I faced, I had to be a fighter. I had to be relentless, just like David in the Bible who saw himself as a king even when he was enslaved and in shambles. His own father did not believe in him. What David had was God and faith. Honestly, that's really all we need. Even when we are not in the positions in life we would like to be, we have to be able to see the royalty within ourselves.

I became more self aware of the fact that innerly I was lacking even though on the outside I appeared perfect. I learned the importance of walking in confidence while struggling inwardly. When I felt down, I looked to the sky and prayed. I found that in self-discovery, it is okay to work on yourself inwardly while simultaneously building yourself up for where you want to be in life. Too often when we are in a dark place in our lives, we tend to sit in that darkness. We sit there so long that we forget what we are working towards. We should be working towards being the better versions of ourselves. We should be battling the unknown. We should be battling our past. And most importantly, we should be fighting to get to our future. We may not get to our future in one piece. Our hearts may be broken, and our souls may be in constant battle from the demonic world, but we are going to get there. It is up to us on how we get there.

As I was growing to find who I am, I researched spirituality, and I found that spiritual inequities affect us one way or another, either in the spiritual realm or on the surface of our lives. God does not make judgements on us for what our ancestors have done the way we unconsciously force judgement on ourselves. What I mean is that we are subconsciously battling with unresolved issues from past events that have nothing to do with us individually. Sometimes we find ourselves battling with issues our ancestors have left for us to resolve in order for these generational patterns to not trickle down to our children. It can be domestic violence, it can be divorce, or it can be a history of molestation in the family. Whatever that spirit or energy is, we have to work hard at making sure it doesn't affect the next generation. In order to control our lives, we must learn how to control these spiritual energies. If we do not learn how to control these energies, they will control us.

I was a couple months old when my father and mother decided to separate. My mother, then a single parent, tried her best to manage in this new world alone as a Haitian immigrant. She was kicked out of her father's house for shaming the culture by having a child without being married. She found herself on her own. Shortly after, when I was two years old, she met my stepfather. He was lost as well and would drink often to numb his pain. His drinking would then fuel his anger and he would become extremely violent. He would hit my mother with anything he could find. He was extremely verbally and physically abusive. I grew up in a toxic environment where I did not see a healthy relationship. My stepfather would beat my mother almost daily. He would damage furniture and then be out on the front porch drinking beer after beer until the cases were gone. He would barely keep a job, so a lot of the financial burden was on my mother.

Even after my mom left that situation when I was six, her pain (energy that was not properly resolved) had her to end up in a situation that was worse. My mother's new relationship was even more violent. Not only would he hit my mother brutally, but he would attack me and my siblings as well. We would come into an environment that was unpredictable, violent and hopeless. The only love we would get in that type of environment was through my mother. She was a loving mother. She would give us plenty of hugs and kisses and she would tell us non-stop that we could be and achieve anything we wanted to. A home cooked meal was prepared almost every night unless she was extremely tired from working her two jobs.

Me not receiving the proper love from a man from birth affected how I viewed men for a long time. Those feelings of distrust did not only affect me in my relationships with men, but with God as well.

I was only four years old when my step-aunt allowed her sons to rape me. From then, my worldview was skewed. The experience implanted fear and anger and gave birth to distrust. The lifeline to distrust is our own unconscious thoughts. Our unconscious thoughts cause us to see people and the world differently even when we are not aware of it. It becomes part of our identity, and we do not even notice it until something occurs to trigger those feelings of distrust.

Thankfully, when I was six years old, the abuse stopped after my mother found evidence of sexual abuse on my body. When my mother confronted my step aunt, she nonchalantly stated that little girls should experience sex. *Was this something she experienced as a child? Was her evil spirit thriving through her?* I will never know, but I do know this: She changed the trajectory of my life forever.

The sexual abuse quickly turned into shame and guilt, and I felt like the black sheep of the family. Everyone knew something was wrong with me but could not quite figure it out. I would display sexual acts in our home, not fully understanding what I was doing. I was just acting out what had happened to me. Back then, without counseling available for my family because at the time we could not afford it, I was left to figure it out on my own.

Faith was a major part of my household. My mother made sure we went to church often. At a young age, I understood spirituality and felt a connection with a higher power. It gave me a sense of hope in many hopeless situations. The older I got, faith also gave me a sense of resentment. I often looked at God as the man who allowed things to occur in my life that shouldn't have. I blamed God for a lot.

It is strange that you do not understand the effects of your past until you enter into a relationship. When you are in a romantic relationship or even a friendship, this is when you begin to see the effects of your past. I met my ex-husband in college. He was charming, talented, and full of love. We clicked immediately. We fell in love. In that union is where I saw a lot of my past manifest. I began to get easily angered for the smallest things. Soon, my relationship would take a bitter turn into a trail of resentment and pain. I didn't understand what it was to keep a marriage together.

It took me years to understand why and how to disassociate my past from my present, and that affected everyone around me. The spirit of separation was all too normal to me. I didn't understand a relationship without chaos. The mind has a way of controlling your behaviors. When we are not aware of our thoughts, they will consume and control us. That's what my thoughts did. At a young age, I learned that love was not normal, and that's what I embodied. I did not fully understand why I was behaving the way I was until I spent some time alone. Spending time alone created a level of awareness. I was able to clear my busy mind and slow down and think. It involved sitting with myself in constant prayer and awareness. I knew from there, my spiritual journey had just begun.

Ephesians 5:13-14 (AMP) "But all things become visible when they are exposed by the light, for it is light that makes everything visible. For this reason He says, "Awake, sleeper, and arise from the dead, and Christ will shine upon you and give you light."

CHAPTER 3

Self-Love vs. Self-Care: How They're Different and How to Practice Them Both

Webster defines self-love as an appreciation of one's own worth and value. Mason Olds once stated, *"Often we are reluctant to promote **self-love** mostly because we confuse it with selfishness. Since we are humans, we ought to have a healthy love for ourselves; it is from this fount that love flows out to others."*

When people think about checking on themselves, most tend to forget to think about the part that needs them the most: their inner selves. It is important to have a connection with your soul and to take time to meditate and listen to what your inner being is telling you. ***John 14:20 (ERV) says, "On that day you will know that I am in the Father. You will know that you are in me and I am in you."*** This verse clearly states that God dwells inside of us, which means that we have the capacity to reach any goals and be as whole as we would like because He lives in us. All we have to do is call on Him and build a stronger bond and connection with Him. We have to understand that our source is not outside of us, but inside of us.

When I suffered with low self-esteem, I looked a lot to other people to validate who I was. I wanted them to believe I was smart. I wanted them to believe I was attractive or even cool. My bruised ego needed the empty compliments. But when I got to understand God, I learned that HIS approval was all I needed.

Building a connection with God means talking to Him and spending time in the Bible and worshipping God as much as possible. The more you are connected to God, the less fear you will have, and the more you will grow as a person. I believe that people are limited simply because they are not aware of what they have within them or around them. Just as God is within us, our ancestors are walking with us every day. They are like guardians watching us and protecting us. They are there as well if you call and pray to them. Wayne Dyer stated, *"If we knew who walked with us every day, we would not live in fear."*

The inner self is something we all have to work on every day in order to enjoy life to its fullest. It is easy to lose who you are in the day to day busy lifestyle. Therefore, it is imperative to check on yourself. In order to be able to check on yourself, you must learn to be fully present with your thoughts, feelings, and spiritual self. We must make an effort to dedicate time to be alone with ourselves. This is when we can listen to what our thoughts and what our hearts are saying. This means becoming one with ourselves and understanding who we are in the world and in Christ. What I mean is if you do not deal with your life, your life will deal with you, and you will lose control. What eventually happens is we "all of a sudden" suffer from anxiety, depression, and other mental health issues because we have not dealt with any of our issues. We are just existing and not living. Well, it's time to live! Our ancestors came from a time where life was much simpler. They were not bogged down with our advanced, fast-paced lifestyles. They had more time to reflect and sort out their emotions. They were not bombarded with a fast-paced life. They were more focused on the now and the day-to- day aspects of life. It is time to slow down a little to focus on our physical and emotional selves before it is too late.

In order to do that we must work on self-care. There are several forms of self-care, and according to Psych Central, self-care is defined as any activity we do deliberately to take care of our mental, emotional, and physical health. Although it's a simple concept in theory, it's something we very often overlook. Good self-care is key to improved mood and reduced anxiety. It's also key to a good relationship with oneself and others. I have experienced so many people who tend to put themselves last, and what happens is that they no longer have equity to give to themselves. It is important that we begin giving ourselves some self-care in order to appropriately take care of those around us.

When I was suffering from panic attacks, it was partly because I was focused on everything else instead of myself. I was in school, taking care of a toddler, and making sure everything was financially well on my own. For me, all of that responsibility without taking the time to figure out what I needed emotionally took a toll on me. I had to take the time out to understand what my mind, body, and soul needed. Meditation helped me with slowing down and listening to my body.

Meditation

One of my favorite authors, Eckhart Tolle, discusses meditation as the next step towards inner peace. Meditation doesn't necessarily mean that you are sitting quietly or exercising deep breathing. Meditation is techniques that are used to shut the noise off from the world of negative thoughts. When we are constantly consumed with our thoughts, it is hard to function effectively. Meditation gives you the opportunity to not focus on the past where depression lives, and to not focus on the future where anxiety lives. It gives you the opportunity to focus on the now. Focusing on the now gives individuals the opportunity to "stop and smell the roses" so to speak. It gives them the leverage to enjoy their loved ones while they can. Most importantly, focusing on the now gives you the opportunity to detach your mind from anger, negativity and irrelevant thoughts.

Anything that can distract you from your current thoughts can be considered meditation. Loud music can be a form of meditation because you are now focused on the lyrics. Watching a comedy show to get you some laughs can be meditation too. Even reading a pleasant book may be a form of meditation. For me, the best form of meditation is spending time with God.

Spending Time With God

Jeremiah 29:13 (NIV) states, "You will seek me and find me when you seek me with all your heart." This bible verse is real for me. The more I find myself indulging in God's presence, the less depression or anxiety I experience. The bible states, in *Isaiah*

12:2 (NIV), "Surely, God is my salvation; I will trust and not be afraid. The LORD, the LORD himself, is my strength and my defense; he has become my salvation." Spending time with God has helped me find peace in my pain and a message in my mess.

Spending time with God entails being in the word, praying, living by the word and building a relationship with God daily. The more I talk to him, the more I see. I am able to see what God has been showing me all along, which is the value I have inside of me. What he has been telling me is that everything that I have been through has a reason. He has been showing me that there was purpose in my pain. Most importantly, I am not here for my own desires. My purpose is to fulfill his vision for my life.

Do you love yourself or are you depending on others to love you?

According to Malidoma Somè, there is a missing link between our African ancestry and our lives. He believes when we are not connected to our ancestors, then there will be repercussions on the quality of our lives. He believes that we cannot move forward into our futures by abandoning our past. No matter how I tried to abandon my past, it had a way of creeping its ugly head back into my present. Seemingly, not having a relationship with my father in the way I wanted forced me to seek love from unhealthy places. I was always seeking something that I never had. What I mean is that I was seeking love, but I did not know what love looked like from a male. Therefore, I found myself in a slew of relationships that lacked love, but were filled with confusion. The relationships lacked love, but were filled with disappointments. The relationships lacked love, but were filled with lust. Once I saw this unhealthy pattern, I decided I needed to stop seeking love from others, and I needed to work on loving myself. Once I started spending time with myself and God, I began to love myself fully. Once I started loving myself, I didn't have to look for love; it started looking for me. We attract what we believe we deserve. Early on in my journey, I didn't believe I deserved love. Therefore, I attracted the opposite, or I pushed love away.

I started doing the work towards making myself a better me. I took time to journal my past relationships and choices I had made. I reset my life by making better choices day by day. I was intentional in my decision making. I decided to make choices that had an impact on my future and not choices that resembled my past. I would ask God if my choices were in alignment with His will and he would answer me and started showing me things without me even asking. Once I was able to love myself, I was able to focus on the other aspects of my life that needed healing, which was my mental capacity.

Mental Care = Self-Care

Mental health is the key to keeping us intact. Mental health is the oxygen to our lungs. It is the air we breathe. If we are not functional mentally, then we cannot function at all. The dictionary defines mental care as *a state of well-being in which every individual realizes his or her own potential.* When individuals take care of their mental health, they are able to cope with normal day-to-day stressors of life. They are able to be productive members of society, functioning in their communities. When people are mentally well, they are able to live their lives to their fullest capacity. When you check on yourself mentally, it means that you care about your well-being. It means you care about your family and friends and about being a productive member of society. The worst thing someone in a potential mental health crisis can do is ignore it.

Over the years, I developed an acronym for C.A.R.E in regard to mental health treatment.

Curious. When individuals first seek therapy, they are mostly curious and nervous about how treatment may go.

Accountability. After they have gone to therapy and the curiosity goes away, they are now held accountable for maintaining and continuing treatment.

Reset. After clients are able to be consistently accountable for their treatment, they are able to reset their old ways of living life. They also have to constantly re-check whether or not they are going into the wrong direction, and if they are, they can reset again.

Empowerment. Lastly, E stands for empowerment. When people are working on bettering their lives, they can remove the stigma that counseling is "crazy" and change it to care.

Physical Care = Self-Care

Not only should we focus on our mental state, we should ensure that our bodies are strong as well. Our ancestors understood the value of the body and took care of their bodies the best way they knew how. Our spiritual, mental, and physical selves all have a function and feed off of each other, essentially operating together as a whole. We must work to ensure that we are treating each component of ourselves as equally important. Some may believe that since they are faithfully talking to God every day and operating in their spiritual selves, they can neglect their physical selves. This is far from the truth. How can God use you if you aren't healthy enough to operate in your gifts? This is why it is just as important to take care of your physical self.

When we view ourselves as less than worthy, we tend to treat ourselves the same way. The devil wants us to believe that we are not worthy of God's grace or forgiveness. This belief is the opposite of what God believes about us. Not believing what God says will cause some to be vulnerable to devaluing their bodies with their actions. Our negative actions are triggered by a negative sense of self. I know this all too well. Seeking validation will have you in compromising situations that will keep you feeling defeated, and most of all, unworthy. I found that when I was in a state of depression or anxiety, my physical self was not a priority. In retrospect, when I made my physical self a priority, my depression and anxiety would gradually go away. Taking care of yourself physically is a must in order to have a healthy mental and emotional state. Physical care not only keeps you fit, but it keeps you disciplined and balanced. Physical health has to be a part of our daily routine. Our physical self can deteriorate if we aren't eating right and exercising regularly. Not taking care of yourself physically is a direct effect of how you feel inside. When we love something, we take care of it. For instance, when we are in love with a precious piece of jewelry, we make sure it is consistently clean, in a safe place, and away from the people we don't trust.

This is how you have to look at your physical self. You must take care of yourself inside and out, keep yourself safe, and stay away from people you do not trust. The way we take care of ourselves from the inside out is by monitoring what we are putting in our bodies. It is imperative that we are mindful of what we are eating and drinking and the medicine we are taking. When taking care of your physical self, it is important to have a level of discipline. This is where some may fall short. They may desire to be fit, but they lack the confidence and discipline to achieve their goals.

1 Corinthians 9: 24-27 (NIV) " Do you not know that in a race all the runners run, but only one gets the prize? Run in such a way as to get the prize. 25 Everyone who competes in the games goes into strict training. They do it to get a crown that will not last, but we do it to get a crown that will last forever. 26 Therefore I do not run like someone running aimlessly; I do not fight like a boxer beating the air. 27 No, I strike a blow to my body and make it my slave so that after I have preached to others, I myself will not be disqualified for the prize."

CHAPTER 4

Career: Expect Setbacks, Don't Lose Focus

When one generation does not get it right, another generation has to pay the price. And I paid the price. I found that a lot of the trauma I faced were patterns that were passed down from my family. But I was, and I still am determined to not let it affect my generation or my children's generation.

My family is full of achievers. I believe since achievement is a part of my bloodline, it was already in me, even when I was failing. When success is a part of your ancestry and life, no matter what hurdle you face, you will overcome. The path to success is already inside of you. It is up to you to believe that the seeds you plant will manifest into something beautiful. When success is a part of you, you have to work diligently to see it manifest. The seed is already planted. It is time for you to water it.

Someone may say, *"Well, I come from people that weren't successful."* My question would be, *"How do you know that?"* When our ancestors were prehistoric, they lived in a time when their history was not recorded. You could be related to a king or queen and you may not know it. It is up to you to tap into the king and queen in you. You can be that shift for your future generations. I encourage you to be like Timothy in the Bible when Paul challenged him to stir up the gifts that were already inside of him. We all have many gifts. Even when people do not want to see the gifts, we still have them.

I will never forget when I thought I landed my dream job at a mental health practice. From the outside appearance of the job, it was well put together and corporate-looking, in a brick building with nice amenities and a beautiful office. Shortly after I started, my dream job began to turn into a nightmare. This is when my path started to ripple into chaos. The atmosphere became toxic and the owners would belittle and degrade people, especially me. I felt like a target. They would often call people dumb, leaving us new counselors feeling incompetent instead of building us up. The owners of the practice were unhappy and egotistical, which trickled down to the employees. Most employees suffered a great deal of sadness. We would look at each other in our cars before the clocks would strike 9 AM and debate why we were even there. The mental health practice was run in a way that promoted division amongst co-workers. Oddly, although this was a black-owned company, they had the mentality that only Caucasians should be in the positions of higher power. The owner would often come in angry and give condescending looks to people, and even talk down to people. The ridicule seemed to get worse and worse. The owner would often shout at me, call me names, and tell me I was incompetent. Instead of training me into a seasoned counselor, he tried to break me down and make me question why I even became a therapist. This felt and sounded all too familiar. Another male in a leadership role was trying to break me down instead of seeing potential in me. This situation did not help my perspective when it came to men. By this point, I had never seen a positive example of a man beyond what I had witnessed on television. By this time, my relationship with my first husband had completely failed, and I was in another relationship that was based on his lies and manipulation. The mistreatment on the job often made us therapists ineffective as counselors. My co-workers began to leave left and right. Unfortunately, I had no choice but to stay for about a year because I was a single mother. Not only was I going through depression from working at a job that did not see any value in me as a counselor, but I was facing motherhood alone. While all this was happening, one day in the midst of turmoil, my mother came to me and told me she had a dream I was in big trouble. She didn't know it yet, but I knew. I was pregnant again, almost eight years after having my first child. This time, by someone who lied about being married.

Again, I brought more shame on my family. During my pregnancy, I harbored anger and resentment towards my daughter's father because he was dishonest. One day, I was called into the office by the owner of the mental health facility. He looked at me and said what I had done was a mistake. He talked about overstepping boundaries and that I should not have become pregnant. With tears in my eyes, I had nothing to say. I went back the next day upset, but determined to regain my mental strength.

"How can you judge **me***?" I said. "How can someone like you, who treats everyone so poorly, and behaves with such evil judge* **me***?"* I also mentioned the child he too had out of wedlock. He retaliated by firing me the very next day. I was five months pregnant.

I felt that this was the worst time of my life because I was constantly sad. Not only because of pregnancy was I sad, but it was because I was facing it all alone. Well, at least I felt like I was alone. One day as I was walking home, I heard an angel whisper to me, *"This will all work out for your good."* I knew I wasn't talking to myself because of all of the fear, anger, and resentment I harbored. After I heard that, a sense of peace came over me. Even with nothing to really show for myself, I had peace. God was with me all along.

Create a Vision for Your Life

It's time to find what your heart bleeds for. This could be something that was unfinished from the past that you were sent here to fulfill. The easiest way to find what your heart bleeds for is to find out what you would do for free if you had to. When finding your niche, don't look for monetary value. Look for purpose. Purpose is what is going to drive you, even when you don't have the strength to drive yourself. People may say, *"Well I have a job that does not allow me to work for my passion."* Well, it's time we make time for what we are passionate about. It's time to find your niche. Or, maybe it is time to take a leap of faith, strategize, and leave the job that is holding you back. Remember there is no room for faith and fear. You have to have faith. I was forced into my leap when I was fired from my job. It was a blessing in disguise. The only regret I have was not believing in myself and not leaving the mental abuse on that job sooner. When you are actively looking for your purpose, it will eventually find you. Things may be looking terrible from the outside, but your passion is on its way.

It is important to create a vision for your life. With purpose there is vision. Vision is what keeps all of the unnecessary things out. When we have a vision, we do not waste time on anything that has nothing to do with our purpose. We begin to eliminate frivolous friends and activities and, in a nutshell, anything that wastes our time. Creating a vision takes time and we do not have time to waste.

Staying focused on how you would like to see your future is key. When we are focused, we don't care if we get fired, we don't care if no one is supporting us, and we don't care what it looks like right now. When we are focused, we are looking for the end result, knowing that in the beginning, and even in between, it may not look like what we would want it to.

A lot of people look for success for the wrong reasons. Some look for it for money, and some look to success for promotions and to be seen and known. But when you are looking for the right reasons, it will always benefit you in the end. The value will always outweigh the egotistical reasoning. Many people often wonder why millionaires have as much money as they have and aren't happy.. Well, my answer is: Value isn't in money; value is in purpose. Purpose and passion are embedded in us, it was embedded in us even during a time money was not even thought of. This is why money cannot make you happy. Your sense of self, love, and value is what makes you truly happy. Our ancestors lived without money; they depended on the direct connection with the earth and sky, with the herbs and animals, with the water and weather. They found purpose through life.

Often, people are afraid to be different and step out of their comfort zones, which is what keeps them stagnant. The danger in being stagnant is that your lineage will have to fulfill your journey one way or another, whether you do or not. The problem is, what price will they have to pay if you do not fulfil the purpose of the family? Don't be afraid to be different. We are custom-made by God. We were born to be different. We live in such a modern-day, hyper speed life that takes away from our accessibility to be calm and centered with our spirituality and direct contact with God. Our ancestors would often talk to God for the things they needed and he was there to answer directly. Our connection to God was through what he supplied us here on earth and we used it to get what we needed.

What I am saying to you is you do not need much to fulfill your purpose. What you need is already here. It is already inside of you. It is clearly stated in **Romans 4:17 (NKJV), "(as it is written, "I have made you a father of many nations") in the presence of Him whom** he believed--God, who gives life to the dead and calls those things which do not exist as though they did;"*

Understand Your Reason Why

When we understand that we are the prize, it is easy to understand our value. My value was given to me by God. Once I understood that, I got to understand my purpose, my reason for being on this earth. When I realized that my mental, emotional, and inner self needed to be whole, I realized I had a life work to fulfill. I first had to deal with my trauma. Then, I had to deal with my mind. Then, my physical self. I knew early on that due to my trauma, I wanted to be in the "helping" profession. At first, I wanted to be a nurse. Then it changed to an educator. Now, I'm a counselor. I knew God placed me in counseling to do even more work.

I was at a women's retreat for church when God told me to tell my story about my trauma from childhood. I was scared, but I followed his directions and orders, even though I did so hesitantly. As I was telling my story about being violated as a child, I looked up and saw so many other women in the room in tears. At the end of the day, a woman slipped me a note. When I opened it, the note said, *"Your story is my story."* I will never forget that day. It was at that moment that I felt aligned with God. After listening to God, I found my purpose. My "reason" is to help other women.

Proverbs 11:14 (AMP) says, "Where there is no [wise, intelligent] guidance, the people fall [and go off course like a ship without a helm], But in the abundance of counselors, there is victory." In other words, one main way God will help you find your purpose is through others.

CHAPTER 5

Religion versus Spirituality

For a long time, I struggled with finding what best fit me--spirituality or religion. Growing up in a Baptist church, it seemed like religion was so much harsher on humanity. Well, it seemed like it was harsh on me. I felt like I would be condemned for every little imperfection that did not please God, like the fiery pits would take me away for my sins at any moment. Webster defines religion as *a specific set of organized beliefs and practices, usually shared by a community or group.* Spirituality is defined as more of an individual practice and has to do with having a sense of peace and purpose. Although my mom rarely went to church as an adult, she wanted to ensure that her children had a firm foundation in faith like she did as a child growing up in a Catholic school in Haiti. She would make our breakfast and watch us while we got picked up by the Baptist church van on Sundays. I never really asked my mom why she did not want to attend church, but as I got older, I understood her reasoning. It was because church folks could be some of the messiest people in the world, meaning they want to praise God on Sunday and gossip on Monday. Mom did not feel this way about everyone, but most people were this way in her eyes. As a child, my experience was a good one, and I always had an eagerness to hear the stories in the bible and understand more. My mom wanted her children to go to Catholic school just like her, so my siblings and I ended up going to St. Peters Elementary School in Pleasantville, NJ. Going to a Baptist church on weekends then experiencing the Catholic religion, I quickly understood how different the cultures were. In the Baptist church, we would feel the Holy Ghost and holler and sometimes fall out. We weren't afraid to praise God either. But in Catholic school, it seemed to be more quiet and they would pray to statues like Mary, mother of Jesus, something not practiced in Baptist church. Growing up between both churches, I found myself practically practicing both faiths. I would pray with rosary beads, pray to saints (things I adopted in Catholic church), and sometimes catch the holy ghost on Sunday. Even in that situation, I understood that even though both faiths were extremely different, they worshipped one God and loved God.

I always knew God was real. Growing up in the Haitian culture, I heard all of the scary stories of voodoo and soul possessions. With most stories, I overheard my grandmother talking about the consequences of voodoo because she was either there or saw someone that had some form of bad luck because of voodoo. I have heard of people going to the voodoo doctor to harm someone they did not like, even their own family member or friend. This could be because of something they may have wanted from them, whether that was money or their happiness. I've heard other stories of people using voodoo to wish bad health on people or make them lose their businesses or lose money. Although a lot of people in the Haitian community practice voodoo, I have also heard that when you practice evil it comes with curses. It is not uncommon for people who practice voodoo to end up worse than the person they were trying to cause harm to.

My mother would always say, *"If there's a devil at work for evil, then there's a God at work for good."* In Haiti, there are two main practices: voodoo and Catholicism. Catholicism was something the slaves adopted from the French when they ruled the little island of Haiti. Therefore, it is not uncommon for people to integrate voodoo and Catholicism when they are doing their rituals. In fact, most voodoo rituals start off with prayers from the Roman Catholic church. In Haitian voodoo, believers will pray and perform animal sacrifices to feed and beckon the spirits. Then, they dance until a spirit takes over their bodies. According to *The National Geographic*, this is either to heal them or offer them some advice.

In doing my own research, I found that there were both good priests and dark sorcerers called bokor. The bokor act like some sort of religious policemen and may put curses on people. In today's culture, we mainly hear about the dark sorcerer, and that was all I heard growing up. As for me, I decided to stay away from voodoo in general. It was nothing I cared to practice, for the bible says, in **Leviticus 19:31 (AMP), "Do not turn to mediums [who pretend to consult the dead] or to spiritists [who have spirits of divination]; do not seek them out to be defiled by them: I am the Lord your God."**

Me being defiant and curious in my spiritual journey, I did want answers and I did seek out psychics, especially after the passing of my young friend, Jessica. She was a bright, vivacious creature, full of life and ambition, but Jessica was a fighter. It would not be uncommon for her to get into a fight multiple times in a club or bar, and that is partly what caused her to leave the club in a frenzy that night after she was involved in a fight and ended up in a car accident.

I recall going into the psychics place and the psychic looking at me and asking me about my dead friend without me even speaking to her. I do believe that some people are blessed with gifts from God, and some may use the gifts pervertedly with bad intentions to harm.

The first time I knew that there was a higher version of myself was in 2012 when I sat with my friend Jessica in her living room. Jessica was the same age as me. We were both single mothers of boys. I admired Jessica for her wit and ambition. We were both educated and wanted more out of life. She eventually pursued her Masters degree and had big plans for the future. Although she was on the right path, she had her demons. Jessica was a slim, brown skinned, height of 5'5" but was not afraid to stand up for herself or speak her mind. I would often try to talk her out of getting into senseless disputes and fights with females over her son's father and focus on better things to come.

That day, Jessica was telling me how excited she was to move to Raleigh to start her new life. All of a sudden, I felt something inside of me tell me to let Jessica know that I loved her. In my mind this did not seem rational. I was thinking, *Why would I tell her this in this moment?* Instead, I gave her a blank stare and it was awkward for both of us. I got up and congratulated her again on her new venture. That was the last time I saw her. A week later, she passed away in the car accident. Once I was able to calm down from the trauma of losing a friend, I was able to connect the dots. My higher self knew I would not see her again. That was why I was supposed to tell her "I love you". I learned two things: God knows our birth date and death date.

I always felt closeness with God. Even as a child, I would talk to him. I also looked at God like a man that would disappoint me, just like the ones in my childhood did. It was difficult for me to separate "man" from the mighty God. As I grew into myself, I found that God is not to blame for the decisions of man because it was he who gave us free will. I also learned that God was not a God of condemnation, but a God of forgiveness. Religion and religious people often temporarily pushed me away from God because they made me believe God was someone who was full of judgement and punishment. As I grew to understand God for myself, I understood that God made us imperfectly perfect. God often sought out the people that were judged, to do and fulfill HIS will, like King David, Timothy, or even Mary Magdalene. Religion is built on community and bringing people together. In other words, religion was made to strengthen or enhance spirituality. Therefore, true spirituality is there to unite people with their authentic and true selves. Sadly, I have met people who have been so caught up in religion that they forget how to invite the spirituality into their lives. In retrospect, when we do not forget the spiritual aspect of faith we become full and find more peace.

Oftentimes, religion encourages negative judgement on self and can be extremely damaging to the human mind/psyche. Spirituality, on the other hand, encourages love and compassion for self and others opposed to judgment and hate. I, too, felt that the closer I got to "religious" folk, the more mess I found myself in. I recall what my pastor said one day. She stated the church is full of people that need healing. That's when I began to understand that what appeared to be a battle with the people in the church was really a battle with their spirits. The bible states, in **Ephesians 6:12 (NIV), "For our struggle is not against flesh and blood but against the rulers, against the authorities, against the powers of this dark world and against the spiritual forces of evil in the heavenly realms."**

I learned that my relationship with God was more important and bigger than religion or making connections with "religious people". But that did not stop my inquisitive mind from exploring other beliefs and spirituality. I wanted to learn about what other believers believed. I found that some people call the spirit of God the holy ghost. Some may call it spirit. Others may call it energy. Energy is the concept of what we put out into the earth and what we get in return.

I found that in the Chinese culture, they call these energies *chi*. In an article I read by Brian Prickle, he describes an elderly man putting on a mysterious performance in a park in China. "Onlookers stood slack-jawed as the gray-haired man effortlessly defended himself against a group of much younger, stronger men, tossing them around the square like ragdolls. The old man was a master of chi energy; he claimed to possess an invisible force, which he could project at will from inside of his body. The puzzled onlookers continued to stare as the old master took on three, four, even six men at once without displaying the slightest bit of strain. He brushed them aside with a simple sweeping motion from his hand as if he were protected by a force field. The act looked supernatural, yet the master explained that anyone is capable of harnessing this power."

I truly believe we can harness any power we would like because the power of God is inside of us.

God is With You and Me

Once we recognize that God is within us, we no longer seek outside validation. We no longer identify ourselves with what people want us to be. Instead, we identify with what God wants us to be. Since God is within us, it is easy to communicate the needs of our hearts with God. All we have to do is ask. The bible states, in **James 4:2 (NIV), "You do not have because you do not ask God."** Don't forget to ask God for your needs. Don't forget to ask God for what he wants for your life. God already gave us the tools we need to be successful and what we need to walk in the purpose he has given us.

In the Chi culture, they also believe that when energy is unbalanced, there will be symptoms of illness and other disruptive patterns in your life.

There were times in my life when I felt unbalanced due to worry or depression, and I did not seek God like I was supposed to. I tried to solve it all on my own. I have learned that without His spirit guiding me, the patterns in my life were disrupted.

In the African culture, it is named the Kundalini energy. The Kundalini energy is naturally a part of us. The belief is that we came into the world to sort out this energy. In the Ngoma African spiritual tradition, they believe that people can be bothered by their ancestors. African spirituality believes that our spirituality goes beyond our lifetime, that it goes as deep as our ancestors, our bloodline, and our lineage. They believe that the spirit influences our everyday lives. They believe that we are intertwined with the elements of the Earth and we carry information that lies dormant or inactive in our DNA. Our karma, the sum of our actions in this life, past lives, and in the lives of our ancestors, impacts our destiny. Thus, the ancestors interrupt us to bring something urgent to our attention, something that needs to be nurtured, addressed, cleared or healed, embraced or achieved. We are because they are. We have the technologies of this life because of their inventions. We benefit from their work and wisdom. We suffer from their mistakes. We are ill of the things that disrupted their lives. Our parents taught us what their parents taught them, and so on and so forth. The dead are still living in the spirit realm. Through the stories we tell, we carry generational curses and generational gifts.

I believe that God has equipped us with what we need to ensure we utilize the gifts he has given us. The gifts of love, hope, and compassion are already there. Don't allow religion to make you believe that you are not deserving of these gifts because of your past or generational curses either. You have the power to break every chain holding you back.

Ephesians 4:22-24 (NIV) "...to put off your old self, which is being corrupted by its deceitful desires; to be made new in the attitude of your minds; and to put on the new self, created to be like God in true righteousness and holiness."

All in all, after all of the spiritual journeys I have researched and traveled, I am more comfortable with the concept of having a stronger relationship with God, directly, rather than through religion, because when it's all said and done, what matters is the relationship I have with God.

CHAPTER 6

Birds of a Feather Flock Together!

You may call them your clique, squad, gang or friend goals. Maslow's Hierarchy of Needs outlines that there are five needs that a human must meet in order to obtain self-actualization. The first is psychological needs. Next, is safety needs. Third, is love and belonging. Fourth, is esteem, and last, but not least, is self-actualization. Maslow's Hierarchy of needs, places the need for love and belonging at number three. Once we have secured our physiological needs and physical safety, we seek out people who can supply us with love and a sense of belonging. We're social creatures, and we crave and desire those close relationships. Everyone needs a safe place to land and people to lean on when there are bad things happening. Believe it or not, our friends determine our lives. Our surroundings affect us one way or another. ***Proverbs 12:26 (NKJV)* states, "*The righteous should choose his friends carefully, For the way of the wicked leads them astray.*"** This bible passage is so profound because the people we choose to surround ourselves with make us better, or they push us away from greatness. Being great means to surround yourself with people who push you to be the better version of yourself. Being the better version of yourself means to be who God has designed you to be and to fully live in your purpose. Always choose to be great.

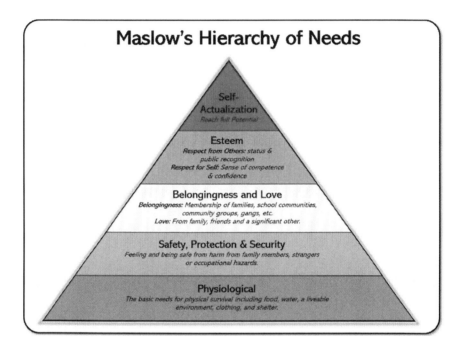

What I found is that negative people come to hold you back and distract you from what God has intended for you. We hold ourselves back from completing and living out our purpose and reaching self-actualization. The way we can work to stop attracting people that want to bring us pain and hold us back from our full potential is to start loving ourselves. When we love ourselves, we start to attract people that love us too. Pain attracts pain. Anger attracts anger. Love attracts love.

Whether we realize it or not, we will attract what we feel about ourselves. If you're asking yourself why you keep attracting un-desirable people, you have to figure out what issues you have not healed from or dealt with. For instance, if you are not attracting love, it could be because you don't believe you completely deserve love and you push it away.

I know this all too well. The adverse experiences I faced early in life taught me that I did not deserve love. It taught me that love was untrustworthy and not real. Sadly, I attracted people that were untrustworthy and not real due to not healing from my past issues. Not healing from my past only caused me to repeat what I experienced in my childhood. These experiences only attracted people that were not able to love me, because at the time, I did not love myself. Attracting the wrong people in our lives gives us a bit of an excitement in the beginning, but ultimately leaves us feeling empty because these people do not add anything in our lives. They subtract until we're zero. We find ourselves giving our time, energy, heart, and love only to get a sense of entitlement from them.

Some people may refute the fact that we attract what we feel about ourselves, but we do. When we do not deal with our past, even if we do attract the right people, we will reject them. Love is energy. When we do not have the right energy inside of us, we tend to remove all of the right things in our lives. Therefore, love is the only energy that attracts love. Don't believe me? Just try loving someone with a damaged heart. It is almost impossible. We have to work towards inner healing in order to attract true love. It's time to change our energy to attract what we deserve.

What Do You Do with These Energies?

In order to make a shift in your energy, it is time to focus on you. It is time to take time to be alone to get some true healing.

You will not realize the type of energy you are attracting until you realize the type of energy you are producing. Not working towards inner peace and throwing things under the rug will cause negative energies to take over your life. The way we get a hold of these energies is realizing that they are there. Energy is in the air. Energy is in what we watch on television. Energy is in the music we listen to. Energy is even in the food we eat. In order to get a hold of energy, you must realize that energy is everywhere and control the energies you allow in your space.

Even in the healing process, we can work towards clearing negative energies. Clearing negative energies can be done by clearing the negative feelings we have about ourselves and clearing those negative thoughts as soon as they enter our minds. As I mentioned earlier, we attract what we feel about ourselves. Therefore, it's time to change the narrative about our feelings and start to invite love in our lives. You may have had an undesirable past, but your future can be bright. Once you believe that you can have a bright future despite all of the negative experiences, you will begin to change the energy you have been holding on to from your past.

What Are You Seeking in Friendships?

Healthy friendships have proven to be a direct correlation to success. The people we allow in our space may have a positive or a negative effect in our lives. Therefore, it is imperative for us to discern if people are intentionally speaking positivity into our lives or intentionally speaking negativity into our lives. When people speak to us, it carries an energy. Have you ever experienced criticism that didn't come from a helpful place, but was instead given to belittle you and make you feel less than? Situations like these give an energy that makes you feel incompetent and an immediate negative feeling. When we carry these energies with us, they affect how we see ourselves and ultimately, it affects our place in the world. This is why it is imperative that we watch what type of people we allow in our space. When people speak into our lives it comes into our minds as a thought. Then, it affects our actions, whether we realize it or not.

I know this all too well. I have had friends bring negativity into my life by making me feel less than, incompetent, and not worthwhile. When these people brought these energies to me, all it did was weaken my confidence. Once my confidence was weakened, all I did was attract people that had a weakened confidence because remember, we attract what we feel about ourselves. A lot of people see the greatness in you and want to hinder you from seeing it in yourself. People will try to stop your greatness because of fear that you will surpass them in success. That's why it is important to seek people that are not threatened by your greatness. You want to seek people who will push you towards success.

It is important that we stick with people who challenge us, not those who make us comfortable with where we are. Fred Devito once said, *"If it doesn't challenge you, it won't change you."* If you are not around people who help break down the fear of failure, rejection and fear, then it's time to find a new flock of birds. To quote Michael Dell of the Dell computer company: *"Try never to be the smartest person in the room. And if you are, I suggest you invite smarter people...or find a different room."* You want to surround yourself with people who offer you new ways to think about your ideas. And doing the same for them–being a sounding board, offering suggestions, or giving them the resources to succeed–will help you succeed as well. Constructive criticism or thoughtful advice can really help you grow. But what you don't want are people who pull you down. You know the type. If you are attracted to friendships that pull you down or away from who you are meant to be, it's time to change your friends. It is time to start inviting energy that is going to lift you up, inspire you, and bring you peace. When we allow people to pour negativity into our lives, we are not pleasing God. We are pleasing the enemy. You have to ask yourself, are you a people pleaser or a God pleaser?

Are You a People Pleaser or a God Pleaser?

The thing about people pleasers is that they never feel fully fulfilled because their pleasing has a sacrifice. The sacrifice could be their happiness, integrity, or their authenticity. In retrospect, when you are a God pleaser, your goals and visions are in alignment with what he wants for your life, not with what people want for your life. It is important to be a God pleaser.

I struggled with being a people pleaser. This came about when I did not have a strong sense of self, and I needed people to validate me. I needed acceptance. That is when I found that the greatest validation is the one we can give ourselves. The best acceptance is when you can accept who you are inside and out. Once I became more whole, my need to be a people pleaser faded, and I wanted to please my inner being. God lives inside of you and me. Therefore, we should want to please God.

Pleasing people instead of pleasing God will have you doubting your intuition because a lot of times, we are only seeing people through the lens of what we would like them to be in our lives. We're not looking at who they truly are. In the past, I have overlooked certain people's characteristics because I wanted to believe that these people were good people. I recall hanging out with someone and something deep inside of me knew that person was not right. I would ignore this feeling of mistrust and try to give that person a chance only to be disappointed and truly hurt by them. If something inside of yourself is telling you something is wrong every time you are around someone, chances are your gut is right. I found that the more I sought to please God, my level of discernment, when it came to what people I wanted in my life, drastically improved. I have met people who ultimately pushed me to do more professionally because they believed in me and saw potential in me that I did not recognize in myself. These were friends that were there not realizing they were building me up through telling me how much of an inspiration I had been to them. Hanging around people that have accomplished more than I have, telling me that I have the ability to achieve what they have and more has been a blessing. It is all about your flock. Is your flock building you up or breaking you down?

Proverbs 13:20 (KJV) "He that walketh with wise [men] shall be wise: but a companion of fools shall be destroyed."

CHAPTER 7

Let Go!

*T*he past has a way of holding us back from who we are meant to be. We are trapped by our past when negative memories replay in our minds and we allow them to be our narrative. These negative memories may hold people back from accomplishing things in the future due to fear of a negative event occurring again. It is time to change our stories by changing the negative thoughts we're telling ourselves. People tend to be bogged down with guilt, pain, and resentment. Many of us struggle with receiving forgiveness because we haven't forgiven ourselves. If God can forgive us of our past, why can't we? ***Hebrews 8:12 (NIV) states, "For I will forgive their wickedness and will remember their sins no more."*** If God is willing to forgive us, why can't we forgive ourselves?

It's Time to Let Go!

It can be difficult to let go of our past mistakes and focus on our present and future. Therefore, it is important to work on forgiving and letting go. If not, there is no room for growth and change. However, the Lord desires that His people walk in the freedom that His forgiveness provides. We have work to do for the Lord so we must receive His forgiveness.

Resist Dwelling on Past Mistakes

"Forget the former things; do not dwell on the past." Isaiah 43:18 (NIV)

Satan is the mastermind of bringing our past mistakes to the forefront of our thoughts. He tends to remind us right before we are ready to take steps of faith, but we must resist dwelling on our past mistakes and continue to speak the word of God to opposing thoughts. My thoughts seemed to always have a way of holding me back from reaching my highest self. I would have thoughts of not being worthy enough. I would have thoughts of feeling like I was not smart enough or good enough to be who God had truly desired me to be. These thoughts would cause me to have panic attacks and delay me from reaching goals I put in place for myself. In order for me to stop these thoughts, I had to take time to change the narrative I was telling myself. I would repeat to myself, *"Despite it all, I am worthy."* Our past has a way of making us feel like it's our fault we experienced the trauma we experienced, but it's not our fault! Trauma may be a part of our journey, but it doesn't define who we are.

We Are Our Own Worst Critics

We tend to be the harshest on ourselves. It is time to remember that we are not made perfect and we will fall short of what God wants for us. The great thing about mistakes is that we can pick up the pieces and learn from our mistakes. Instead of being harsh on ourselves, let's anticipate the fact that we will make mistakes and there will be tough times in our lives. Once we anticipate the storm, we will not run from it, but we will run towards it, ready to fight, because we are prepared for trials. And we can fight against almost anything once we know who is on our side. God is in all of us, and he is there to protect us. Stop criticizing yourself and reach towards the calling on your life.

Reach Towards Your Calling Instead of Focusing on Past Mistakes

"...But one thing I do: Forgetting what is behind and straining toward what is ahead, I press on toward the goal to win the prize for which God has called me heavenward in Christ Jesus." Philippians 3:13-14 (NIV)

It's important for us to move towards our calling instead of focusing on our past mistakes. We don't have eternity on this earth to accomplish God's will in our season. By letting go of the past and keeping busy with God's work, we will grow in our faith and be a significant part of helping others grow as well. Believe it or not, we walk through various situations in our lives in order to later help other people grow and become better versions of who they already are.

Renew Your Relationship with God from Your Past Mistakes

"Create in me a pure heart, O God, and renew a steadfast spirit within me." Psalm 51:10 (NIV)

Do not allow your mistakes to separate you from God. Use your mistakes as a way to gain wisdom and grow closer to God. God doesn't want us to run away from Him—He wants us to run towards Him. He is our Father in heaven who loves us with a great and everlasting love. Allowing God to be in control and releasing our worries to him can be difficult for most. Here are some ways to let go and let God.

- **Start each day by giving it to God.** Do not take yesterday's mistakes and pain into the new day. Mentally work on letting go of every single worry, doubt, fear, mistake, and anxiety from your mind each morning.
- **Give it to God by starting each day with prayer.** Speak to God. Yes, the day is full of responsibilities, but first talk to God. Always acknowledge Him first. Tell Him that you are thankful for Jesus' sacrifice for your life. Invite God's Spirit to guide you that day. Before you talk to anyone, speak to God first. He will set each day on the right path.
- **Give it to God by starting each day with Scripture.** Open your Bible and read where you left off from the previous day. Look through your emails and find encouraging verses that are sent to you. The Bible has a way of giving us hope and a sense of freedom.

- **Give it to God by surrounding yourself with encouragement.** You will never make it alone. You need to have people who speak truth, love, and peace into your life. You can also listen to podcasts, read books, watch videos, and listen to Christian music that boosts your faith and encourages your spirit.

- **Give it to God by renewing your mind continually.** The world will constantly try to add worries to your day, so it is important that you constantly work and maintain your spiritual growth. Continually surrender those worries to God. You have to trust that God is with you always. When you let go, you can fully rest in His strength and release yourself of burden.

Remember Your Cleansing from Past Mistakes

It is important that we work towards living a purposeful life, opposed to living in the past where mistakes live. When living in the world, it is easy to engage in a sinful life, but it is important that when we are moving away from sin, we become more like Christ and not like "man." Being like Christ will help us reach our fullest potential. We will live a life that is pleasing to God. I have fallen victim to living like the world, and all it did was hurt me. Mercifully, we can change, and God will forgive.

Thank Goodness for God's Grace

God's grace reminds us that we do not need to hold on to things that were meant to hold us back. His grace reminds us that he will forgive us, but we have to be willing to forgive ourselves. God's grace gives us the hope that we tend to lose the more we indulge in sin. His grace is the perfect ending to a tragic beginning, but in order to get to that ending, we must know who God is in our lives. We must no longer be trapped by our thoughts and we must learn to set ourselves free from the bondage we put on ourselves. We put ourselves in situations then make it seem like we are unable to get out of it. It is time to be free and let go!

I have met so many people who were afraid of letting go, not knowing what was on the other side of no longer holding on. It's almost like holding on is more comforting than anything. In order to let go, we have to get uncomfortable. A lot of times on the other side of familiarity there is a life of freedom. Have you ever seen anyone bungee jump? You can see the initial fear in their eyes. Then, when they let go, there's a freedom that's unimaginable. I've never personally been bungee jumping, but I have heard from people that have gone multiple times. They all say there is always an initial level of anxiety. Then, it goes away after they let go and release. In life, there will be times when we have to constantly let go, release, and start over. It may be scary every time, but well worth it to let go.

There is a lot of danger in not letting go. One danger is that you look back in life and regret not taking another route, not knowing what life could have had in store for you if you would have let go. Another regret is that you don't see where your full potential could have been. Being trapped in a cage sometimes makes you feel like you can't fly to new heights, but once you set yourself free, you see that you can fly and go anywhere in life. When a baby bird is trapped in a cage, it does not know it can fly until it is set free from the cage. What cage are you trapped in? Is it trauma, past failures, or people letting you down? Well, it's time to open that cage and let go! It took a while for me to realize that I hold the key to the cage that I was trapped in. In order to be free in my heart I first had to realize I was trapped in my mind. I had trouble letting go of the fact that my father was not around. I had to let go of the fact that I was molested. I had to let go of the fact that I had a failed marriage. I had to let go of the belief that I did not deserve love. Letting go allowed me to fill myself with love and it allowed me to receive love.

*Proverbs 3:5-6 (NIV) "Trust in the LORD with all your heart and lean not on your own understanding; *[6]*in all your ways submit to him, and he will make your paths straight."*

CHAPTER 8

Stop Blaming God and Start Thanking God

Our relationship with God before we were introduced to sin was a world of less worry, anxiety, and sadness. We had a sense of assurance and confidence, leaving us to feel shameless before God. Now that we are born to sin, we are more prone to sin, sometimes leaving us to make choices that result in blaming God for some of our path, opposed to thanking Him for not allowing us to stay down the wrong one.

When working on ourselves, we sometimes tend to blame others for our misfortunes. We blame ourselves or even God. It's time to find your truth, and once you do, you will put most of the accountability on yourself. I found myself blaming God for the trauma I experienced in the past. I believed that what I went through could have been prevented if God could have only stopped it. As I have grown, I've found that my traumatic experiences were all a part of a plan to not only enhance me, but to enhance other people. I had to go through it so I could grow through it. In that growing process, I was being prepared so I could share my story and live out my purpose on this earth. Once I saw the beauty in my pain, I was able to share that pain. I was able to walk upright and strong. I was able to believe God's plan for my life. I was able to help those around me. It was time to let go of my past mistakes and forgive myself. Phillipians 2 tells us how to become blameless, innocent, and without blemish, even in the midst of our sinful desires and world. Paul tells us to do "everything without complaining or disputing." In other words, it is teaching us to be thankful. Paul states that our thankfulness will cause us to "shine like the stars" in "the midst of the dark."

A Lifestyle of Thanksgiving

We can appreciate the now by focusing on what is going well in our lives currently. One great thing I know is going well right now for each and every one of us is the fact that we are still alive. Being alive gives us the opportunity to live and fulfill our purpose. It gives us the opportunity to let go of the things holding us back. It allows us to start again. And we always have the chance to start again. We have to remember that we have plenty of chances to show ourselves who we can truly be. We have to learn to be intentional in wanting to learn from our mistakes and make permanent change. We have to literally tell ourselves that we are determined to be better than we were before. That comes with accepting who we were and loving who we are going to become. We have to have a spirit of worship and thanksgiving. Having a spirit of thanksgiving is a lifestyle! If you are constantly suffering with any sin, it is a worship or a thanksgiving issue. This means you are worshipping yourself, someone, or something that may be taking precedence over God. The only way to begin living a life of thanksgiving is to start transferring your energy towards worship and not the sin. In order to accomplish this, follow these steps:

1. **Be Hopeful**. Being hopeful gives us the opportunity to be optimistic despite what we are going through. When we are hopeful we know that we are going to get past the hurt and pain we are experiencing, and we can focus on thanking God in advance for getting us out of the trauma.

2. **Understand that setbacks are a part of the journey.** Without setbacks we are unable to learn how to do things better the next go around. No matter how many setbacks I experienced, I intrinsically knew that I was going to be successful despite what my now looked like.

3. **Continue to praise God.** Praising God gives us the opportunity to change our mindsets. We are not sad or focused on circumstances that are temporary; we are focused on God's promise for our lives. When I lost my job while pregnant with my second child, that setback was a setup for me to make six figures the following year. In that moment, I knew I could not quit, and that I had to keep being hopeful that God would deliver on his promise that all things would work for my good.

I used to listen to my friends and co-workers' trauma and compare mine to theirs. I always felt that my mess was the worst. For example, I recall in grad school sharing stories of past trauma, and my friend distraughtly cried about her father and mother divorcing over 20 years ago. I felt like I wished that was the *only* thing I experienced, and not everything else I'd gone through. I would blame God for putting so much on me. I would ask him many times why I just didn't have a normal childhood without all of the trauma and confusion? The resentment I had for my friends that experienced less trauma did not affect any of my friendships because deep inside, I knew that I was being selfish for believing that my trauma was in a sense more significant than someone else's. As I grew older, I learned that everyone has gone through some form of trauma and it does not matter whether I see their trauma as magnified as mine. It is still trauma and we all have different stories in different parts of our lives. Some may experience hurt as children, and some as teens or adults. And then there are people who have experienced hurt mostly all of their lives. The object is to figure out why you were put on this earth because it makes it easier to comprehend why we should not blame God, but why we should thank him.

Thanking him through the pain and being hopeful is not an easy task.When I began worshipping God instead of the people that caused me harm, there was a weight lifted off my shoulders. I stopped obsessing over the betrayal, the evil, and the manipulation and started focusing on what love was. That is when I began to gain a spirit of love, hope, and thanksgiving. Thankfulness takes your mind off the worry, anxiety, and sadness and puts it on God.

What hinders us from going to God is the idea that we are way too flawed. We feel like we have sinned far too much to help other people, but I have come to tell you that you can be flawed and still have purpose. In fact, your purpose can overrule your flaws. Do not allow your past mistakes to hinder you from achieving your purpose. Walk in faith and showcase the purpose God gave you when you were in your mother's womb. Everything is already inside of you.

Seeking the Truth

The enemy wants to keep us sad, angry, and full of shame. When we seek the truth, it is easier to stop the shame and start thanking God. It seems we spend most of our lives seeking the truth about who we are. We sometimes think we can find the truth through our relationships, through our careers, or through how people identify us. As we continue living our lives without knowing the truth about ourselves, our truth seems to get hidden with every adversity we experience until we get to the root of the lie. What happens is, through our hardships and experiences, we add another layer over the truth because of fear and the disbeliefs we have accepted. But once we continue to walk through our journeys, those layers we put on ourselves start to peel off one by one. We, then, continue to walk in our purpose and journeys and find that the truth was inside of us all along.

Our truth is not what people call us when we walk into our corporate jobs. It is not the names we have given ourselves. Our truth lies in who we are without the titles. We are spiritual beings.

It's hard to accept our spiritual selves because we tend to focus on our physical selves. Solely focusing on myself without God's direction left me broken, and I felt all alone in the poor decisions I was making in my life. Until I figured out that I was never alone, even in my mistakes, God was with me. I did not have to fight my physical self. Instead, I had to focus on making my spiritual self stronger. I found that I was fighting flesh with flesh when I needed to fight my flesh with my spiritual self. Like the younger version of me, I was too preoccupied with my physical self, my looks, and being accepted by people. When I was solely operating in the physical I was weak and easily manipulated. It is important that we understand that we must be strong spiritually. Who we are spiritually needs to be a priority! Every day we are fighting a spiritual world we know nothing about. The bible states in ***Ephesians 6:12 (NIV), "For our struggle is not against flesh and blood, but against the rulers, against the authorities, against the powers of this dark world and against the spiritual forces of evil in the heavenly realms."***

The truth can be found in our spiritual selves because this is what we are really fighting every day—not our spouses, not our co-workers, not the neighbor down the street, or the friend who tried to backstab us. We are fighting the spirit world and in order to keep our physical selves intact, we must work on our hearts. That's where the truth lies and that's where God lies. He is inside of us.

Romans 8:28 (NIV) "And we know that in all things God works for the good of those who love him, who have been called according to his purpose."

CHAPTER 9

Step Outside Your Bubble

We are all born into "a bubble". Our bubble could be our cultures, environments, or the way we were raised. There is nothing wrong with being inside your bubble because everyone wants to be able to identify with something. Our bubble sometimes keeps us feeling secure, but there are times that our bubbles will keep us trapped and not willing to experience new things. It is easy to get caught up with the day to day and forget that we should work on stepping out and making real things happen for ourselves. Our lives sometimes become routine. We go to work, take care of the kids, husband, and household and turn around and do it again, day after day. But are we working on our true calling? When I say step out the bubble, this means talk to people, learn new cultures, and learn how to fit in what really makes you happy. I have encountered people who feel guilty because being a wife and mother is not enough for them. They want more, and it's because it is a true gift to be a wife and mother, but that is not their purpose. Most of the time, the way we get to our purpose is by stepping out of our comfort zones. It is by not following the same paths we have been following, but ultimately trying things that we are afraid of, like stepping out and really fulfilling our calling. Let's pop the bubble and step out and be who we are called to be. I love to use the acronym BUBBLE to describe how to step out of the bubble.

Be Bold. When we step out to become our true selves, there's a boldness that comes with it, and a confidence that is undeniable.

Uncomfortability. It's time to get uncomfortable. Our next step to success is outside our comfort zones.

Believe. Without a shadow of a doubt, believe that you will succeed. There will be times when we fail, but failure only takes us to a place where we begin to learn to lean towards succeeding.

Break negative thoughts and cycles. We sometimes stay trapped in our bubble because we fear that people will judge us for wanting something new. It is time to put yourself first and break these stagnant generational cycles.

Love yourself enough to know that you are worthy, and that you're enough to go after your dreams. Sometimes we stay stagnant because in the past, someone showed us or taught us that we were not worthy of more than who we are. You are worth everything because God loves you.

Even though life taught you that success cannot happen to you and for you, it will. Even though you may feel like you are far behind, God can put you in the front line at any time.

Being bold means you know that trials and tribulations will come, but you don't let that stop you from going to the next level. When we expect setbacks, it does not hold us back for long, but it pushes us to want to achieve and accomplish more. I do not know a single person who has achieved long lasting success without a setback or failure. It's important to know that it will all be a part of the process.

In order to step out of your bubble, it is time to get uncomfortable. So many people are literally trapped in jobs, careers, and even relationships that they are not happy with, and they truly will not be happy unless they step out of what makes them feel comfortable. I always wanted to be a public speaker, but I had a fear of speaking in public. At times this fear was debilitating, sometimes leaving me anxious and stuttering over my words when I practiced in front of people. But I learned that in order for me to get better at what I wanted to achieve, I had to step outside of my comfort zone. I had to learn to get comfortable with first being uncomfortable. I had to learn to speak in front of complete strangers. When I had my first speaking engagement, the Spirit spoke **Psalm 118: 6 (KJV, NIV)** to me, saying, *"The Lord is on my side, I will not be afraid. What can man do to me?"* Who we have inside of us is more powerful than anyone on this earth. I walked in with a sense of boldness and confidence and I owned that conference room. It was a rewarding feeling, but I would have never known I would have been great at speaking unless I stepped out of my comfort zone and got uncomfortable.

I have had cycles in my life where I felt unworthy, and I did not believe in or love myself enough to go after my dreams because of people treating me as if I could not achieve my dreams. But there was always something inside of me telling me to push harder, even though I was considered unworthy. When I began to use my past as a push to catapult me to my destiny, I was unstoppable! It is time to stop allowing people, or even your own thoughts, to keep you from what God has given you. Stop looking around expecting people to do things for you and get things done on your own. Everything you need is already inside of you. God said in His word, *"You have not because you ask not."* It is time to ask God to unlock what you already have. When you do, be bold and undeniably confident, and believe. Break negative thoughts/cycles, love yourself, and know that God will provide your needs.

Breaking negative thoughts about ourselves can be difficult at times. The Bible states, in **Proverbes 23:7 (AMP), "For as he thinks in his heart, so is he."** We do not realize how powerful the human mind can be, and when we constantly start thinking negatively about ourselves, it replaces positive thoughts and becomes who we are as a whole. We become our thoughts because our thoughts affect our behaviors, practices, and actions. We have to start looking at ourselves as already accomplishing our dreams. Like I said, we become who we "think" we are so start thinking positivity.Start thinking prosperity. Start thinking happiness. Even when I lacked what some people would call success, I always felt and thought deep down inside of me that I was more than what I was, and that is how I became who I am today. It was through believing what God believed in me all along.

We also have to love ourselves. It is possible to love others so much that we forget about who we are and what God has created us to be. It is time to love ourselves enough to understand that in order to be truly happy we have to love ourselves first. I have met clients who have gotten married or had children and put themselves last, only to find later, when their children were older, that they had fulfilled their roles as parents, but they had never found "their happiness" outside of their bubble. If this sounds like you, I challenge you to both fulfill your duties in the home while simultaneously finding out what makes you happy as well. It is possible to fulfill your dreams and be a great mother, husband, wife, and father as well. You are worthy of happiness. We only have one life to complete our God-given tasks.

I have encountered people who have stayed in their bubble because they feel like their momma, dad, aunts or uncles didn't do anything, so why should they? I am here to tell you that even though they may not have fulfilled their dreams, you can! Even though they made you believe that it is okay to be just like them, you don't have to be! Even though you grew up in poverty, you will be rich. Even though you've seen failure generation after generation, you will be the one to stop that cycle by first stepping out of your bubble.

I have met people that felt hopeless and sometimes felt like God forgot about them, but when they turned that hopelessness into hope and truly started believing relentlessly, resources started coming to them and things started to happen. I will never forget a woman I met at a conference where I was speaking. She had tears in her eyes and she said, *"I want to be a musician so bad, but things are not coming along for me."* Meanwhile, she was the one performing at the conference, playing the piano beautifully, and she performed for her church as well. We are often working on our gifts but want more. What if this is the season of sharpening? The season of practicing? We have to remember that when we plant a seed, it may take a long time to reap a harvest. A delay is not a denial. We have to walk in boldness and believe that things will happen for us according to God's plan. Wait for the harvest.

Ephesians 1:11 (NIV) *"In him we were also chosen, having been predestined according to the plan of him who works out everything in conformity with the purpose of his will."*

CHAPTER 10

Resilience

*R*esilience is defined as *the ability to recover quickly from difficulty.* It is inevitable that we will experience difficulty, but a lot of people have issues with being resilient. Einstein once stated, *"In the midst of difficulty, there is opportunity."* In difficulty, we have the opportunity to learn from our trials and become stronger and wiser, or allow the difficulty to make us fold. With my experience of emotional, physical, and sexual abuse, I decided to not allow it to make me fold. I wanted to come out stronger. I have encountered people that have resented me for my ability to bounce back from such harsh things because they were still stuck in a dark place. There were people who were upset about how happy I was after the divorce, how I bounced back from being fired from my job, and how life threw me some curveballs that I caught and used for my good.

I believe some people have the expectation that once things fail, you should stay on the ground. I say absolutely no to that. It is time to get up and stand up because we do not have a lot of time to fulfill our purpose. The more difficulties we face, the more relevant we become and the more people we will be able to help. Isn't that what life is all about? Going through things and helping those that may be experiencing the things we have overcome? Absolutely!

I have encountered so many people who are at a place of stangnancy because the trauma in their lives made them feel that they literally could not move. They will describe it as wanting to move but something is constantly holding them back, and it's usually the fear of failing again. My mentor, Dr. Myles Munroe, once stated that a trial will come but we don't need to be afraid of the trials; we need to GET READY for them.

I love the eagle because it is one of the wisest birds and there is so much we can learn from the eagle. One of the things that makes the eagle significant is its ability to not fear the storm. Instead of getting away from the storm, it goes towards the storm. It uses the storm to lift higher and uses the pressure of the storm to rise higher in a matter of seconds. The storm helps it glide higher without it having to use its own energy. I challenge you all to use your "storms" as leverage to lift you higher, not keep you down.

I have been through some tough times in my life, but guess what? I got past the storm. The way I used my storms as leverage was by helping others who have felt stuck get unstuck. I have helped people who did not believe, hope and feel again. I helped people who have experienced trauma, like myself, get past it and become stronger from it. I am unapologetically resilient. In most cases, once you get past the storms, you start thanking the storms for bringing you so far. At first, I could not understand why I went through my sexual abuse at such a young age, but now I am thankful because it made me become who I am today.

My dear friend once said to me, *"I believe the enemy will attack*

Made in the USA
Columbia, SC
19 February 2021